JOHN POWELL, S.J.

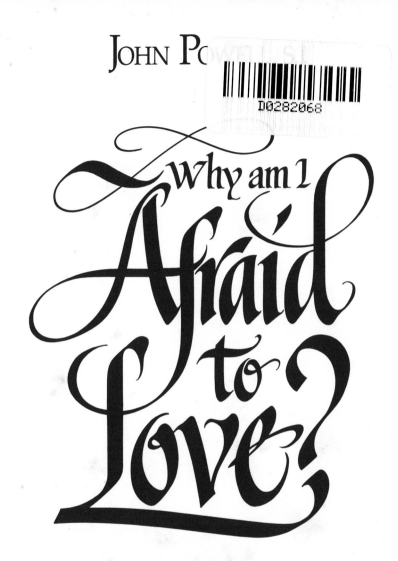

# Why am I Afraid to Love?

## Overcoming Rejection and Indifference

TABOR
PUBLISHING

**Allen, Texas**

Cover design: Karen Malzeke-McDonald

Calligraphy: Sue Bohlin and Bob Niles

Send all inquiries to:
Tabor Publishing
One DLM Park
Allen, Texas 75002

Printed in the United States of America

ISBN 1-55924-278-7

1 2 3 4 5     94 93 92 91 90

# Contents

Beloved,
let us love one another,
because love is of God;
everyone who loves
is begotten by God
and knows God.
Whoever is without love
does not know God,
for God is love.
In this way
the love of God
was revealed to us:
God sent his only Son
into the world
so that we might have life
through him.
In this is love:
not that we have loved God,
but that he loved us
and sent his Son
as expiation for our sins.
Beloved,
if God so loved us,
we also
must love one another.

*1 John 4:7–11*

# CHAPTER ONE

# The invitation to love

The word *religion* is derived from the Latin word *religare*, which means "to bind back." By their practice of religion, people bind themselves back to God who is the alpha (origin) and omega (destiny). To anyone who is familiar with the New Testament there can be no doubt that the essential act of religion and the essential bond between humans and their God is *love*. When Jesus was asked by the Pharisees, "Which commandment in the law is the greatest?" he answered:

> *"You shall love the Lord, your God, with all your heart, with all your soul, and with all your mind. This is the greatest and the*

*first commandment. The second is like it: You shall love your neighbor as yourself."* Matthew 22:36–39

What does it mean to love God with one's whole heart, soul, and mind? I think that Saint John would answer this question by telling us that before we can really give our heart, soul, and mind to God, we must first know how much God has loved us, how God has thought about us from all eternity, and desired to share his life, joy, and love with us. Christian love is a response to God's infinite love, and there can be no response until we have somehow perceived that God has first loved us, so much so that he sent his only-begotten Son to be our salvation.

More than this, God does not simply *have* love; God *is* love. If *giving* and *sharing* with another is the character and essence of love, then God is love. He can acquire nothing because he is God. He needs nothing because he is God. He has all goodness and all riches within himself. But goodness is self-diffusive; it seeks to share itself. So the infinite goodness which is God seeks to communicate, to diffuse, to share itself . . . with you . . . with me . . . with all of us.

We know something of this love in our own instincts to share that which is good and is our possession: good insights, good news, good rumors. Perhaps the best analogy in our human experience is that of the young married couple, very much in love and very much alive because of that love, wishing to share their love and life with new life which it is in their power to beget. But it is even more than this with God, who tells us: If the mother should forget the child of her womb, I will never forget you!

It is precisely this that is the point of most failures to love God truly. Most of us are not deeply aware of God's fatherly, even tender love. It is especially the person who has never experienced a human love, with all of its life-giving effects, who has never been introduced to the God who is love through the sacrament of human love, that stands at a serious disadvantage. The God of love who wishes to share his life and joy will probably seem like the product of an overheated imagination—unreal.

There is no human being who will not eventually respond to love if only that person can realize that he or she is loved. On the other hand, if the life and world of an individual is marked by the absence of love, the reality of God's love will hardly evoke the response of his or her whole heart, soul, and mind.

## False Gods before Us

The God who enters such a life will be a fearsome and frowning idol, demanding only fear of his devotees. The Book of Genesis tells us that God has made us in his image and likeness, but it is our most perduring temptation to invert this, to make God in our human image and likeness.

Each of us has a unique and very limited concept of God, and it is very often marked and distorted by human experience. Negative emotions, like fear, tend to wear out. The distorted image of a vengeful God will eventually nauseate and be rejected. Fear is a fragile bond of union, a brittle basis of religion.

It may well be that this is why God's second commandment is that we love one another. Unselfish human love is the sacramental introduction to the God of love. We must go through the door of human giving to find the God who gives himself.

The Book of Genesis tells us that
God has made us in his image and
likeness, but it is our most perduring
temptation to invert this,

to make God in our human image
and likeness.

Those who do not reject a distorted image of God will limp along in the shadow of a frown. They certainly will not love with their whole heart, soul, and mind. A fearsome, vengeful God is not lovable. There will never be any trust and repose in the loving arms of a kindly Father; there will never be any mystique of belonging to God. People who serve out of fear, without the realization of love, will try to bargain with God. They will do little things for God, make little offerings, say little prayers, and so on, to embezzle a place in heaven. Life and religion will be a chess game, hardly an affair of love.

## Response to God's Love

People who are open to the realization of God's love will want to make some response of their own love. How can they make a meaningful response if this God cannot acquire anything and needs nothing? Saint John points out the place of human response:

> The way we came to know love was that Jesus Christ laid down his life for us; so we ought to lay down our lives for our brothers and sisters. . . . Beloved, let us love one another, because love is of God;

*everyone who loves is begotten by God
and knows God. Whoever is without love
does not know God, for God is love. . . .
No one has ever seen God. Yet, if we love
one another, God remains in us, and his
love is brought to perfection in us.*
*1 John 3:16; 4:7–8, 12*

Meeting God in other humans is the most
costly part of the dialogue between God and
his people. Human nature requires that we
somehow contact God in a bodily or sensibly
perceptible way. In the Old Testament God
came to the Israelites in thunder and lightning
over Sinai; the voice of God emerged from a
burning bush. In the New Testament God's
goodness is even more astonishing: God
becomes a man and is raised in agony on a
cross for you and me. "This is what I mean
when I say I love you." In the Incarnation
God brought his gifts in the earthen vessel of
humanity that he might speak our language
and we might know what he is really like.

Just as God expected people to find him
under the veil of humanity, even when that
humanity was a red mask of blood and agony,
so now he expects people to find him under
other human veils. It will, indeed, cost us a

great deal if we take God seriously on this
point:

> " 'For I was hungry and you gave me food;
> I was thirsty and you gave me drink, a
> stranger and you welcomed me, naked and
> you clothed me, ill and you cared for me,
> in prison and you visited me.'
>
> "Then the righteous will answer and say,
> 'Lord, when did we see you hungry and
> feed you, or thirsty and give you drink?
> When did we see you a stranger and
> welcome you, or naked and clothe you?
> When did we see you ill or in prison, and
> visit you?'
>
> "And the king will say to them in reply,
> 'Amen, I say to you, whatever you did for
> one of these least brethren of mine, you
> did for me.' "    Matthew 25:35–40

The early Christians did not distinguish
our love of God from human love. In fact,
they had one word, *agape,* to describe the one
love that simultaneously embraces the God
of love and the least of their brothers and
sisters.

But all this is old stuff, isn't it? Sometimes
when we grow stale, there is a temptation to
think that it is really God's Word that is stale.

When the dimensions of generous response seem shrunken in us, we are tempted to turn away from the real issue. We tend to look for more practical, relevant issues to discuss.

This is a dangerous thing to do: to avoid confrontation with the real challenge of God's Word. Someday we shall all inevitably meet God. The danger of embarrassment is great. The Lord just might ask as he extends his hands to greet us just beyond the door of death:

*"Where are your wounds?"*

It just might be that, with Saint Augustine, who wrestled a long time before succumbing to grace, we shall have to say:

*"Too late, O Lord, too late have I loved you."*

## The Meaning of Love

Whatever else can and should be said of love, it is quite evident that true love demands self-forgetfulness. Many people use the word and claim the reality without fully understanding the meaning of the word or being able to love to any great extent. This is the test of true love: *Can we really forget ourselves?* There are many counterfeit products on the market which are called love. They are in fact falsely named. We can sometimes label the gratification of our needs "love." We can even do things for others without really loving. The acid test is always the probing question of self-forgetfulness.

Can we really focus our minds on the happiness and fulfillment of others? Can we really ask not what others will do for us, but only what we can do for them? If we really want to love, then we must ask ourselves these questions.

We must become aware that we are capable of using people for our own advantage, for the satisfaction of our deep and throbbing human needs. We can be deluded into thinking that this is really love. The young man who professes to love a young woman may often be deceived into thinking that the gratification of his own egotistical urges really constitutes love. The young woman who finds the voids of her own loneliness filled by the companionship and attention of a young man may well mistake this emotional satisfaction for love. Likewise, the mother and father who anxiously try to promote the success of their children can easily rationalize their desire for the vicarious experiences of success. They might even convince themselves that they are unconditionally loving parents. The critical question always remains that of self-forgetfulness. Does the young man or woman, the mother or father really practice self-forgetfulness, forgoing personal convenience and emotional satisfaction? Do they seek only the happiness and fulfillment of the beloved? These are not merely theoretical questions. The fact of the matter is that, for most of us, our own needs are so very palpable and real to us. Consequently, it is very difficult for the seed to fall into the ground and die to itself before it can live a life of love.

# Human pains in a loveless world

All of us to some extent are enduring agonies of loneliness, frustration, emotional and spiritual starvation. Somehow these pains are radically due to failures in love. The essential sadness of such pain is that it magnetizes the focus of our attention. Pain preoccupies us with ourselves. And self-preoccupation is an absolute obstacle to a life of love.

I once asked a psychiatrist friend of mine, "How can you teach people to love?" His answer was mildly surprising, to say the least. He answered the question by asking one of his own: "Did you ever have a toothache? Of whom were you thinking during the distress of your toothache?" His point was clear. When we are in pain, even if it be only the passing discomforts of an aching tooth, we usually think only about ourselves.

The psychiatrist continued: "This is a pain-filled world in which we are living. And the pains that reside deep in the human hearts around us are much worse than toothaches. We go to bed with them at night and we wake up with them in the morning. Two-thirds of all the hospital beds in this country are now occupied by mental patients. One out of ten Americans has already been treated for mental illness. The pain inside of these poor people simply became too deep and required professional attention. The suicide rate in the eighteen to twenty-one year age group is extremely high. Suicide ranks as the second highest killer in this age group. In the twenty-one to twenty-four year age group, it is the third highest killer. This is a pain-filled world, and so a loveless world, that we live in. Most human beings are so turned in by their own pains that they cannot get enough out of themselves to love to any great extent."

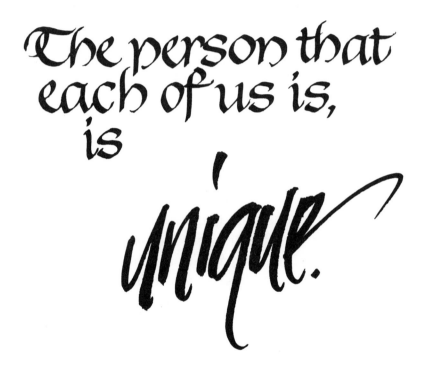

The person that
each of us is,
is

unique.

## Person and Personality

Each of us is obviously a unique and
individual *person.* We sometimes facetiously
remark to others: "After you were made,
God broke the mold." In fact, each of us is
fashioned in a unique mold. There never has
been and never will be anyone exactly like
you or me. However, at the beginning of life
each person is, as it were, like the bud of a
flower or plant: closed. Only when the bud
of the flower receives warmth from the sun
and nourishment from the mothering soil
will it open and expose all of the beauty that
is latent within it. So, too, each person at the
beginning of life must receive the warmth of
human love and the assurance and nourishment of parental affection. This is essential if
he or she is to open and expose the unique
beauty that God has placed within every
human individual.

*Personality,* in the sense that we are using
the word here, is the social manifestation or
expression of *person.* We express ourselves
and our unique personal beauty in various
ways. This process of opening and self-
revelation is what psychologists call the
*dynamics* of human personality.

We know that if the bud of a flower is injured by hostile forces, like an unseasonal frost, it will not open. So, too, those persons who are without the warm encouragement of love, and who must endure the chilling absence of praise and affection, will tend to remain closed in on themselves. The dynamics of human personality will be jammed. And if the dynamics of personality are seriously impeded, the result will be what psychologists call *neurosis.* Although there are many valid descriptions of neurosis, neuroses are commonly recognized in the form of a crippling inability to relate well to others. Neurotic people find it difficult to go out to others and to accept them as they are. They almost always anticipate rejection.

## The First Seven Years of Life

Many of us have been driven by our discomfort to seek professional help from a clinical psychologist or psychiatrist. We are often surprised that the doctor evinces particular interest in the earliest memories of his patients' childhood. It is the unanimous consensus of psychologists that our basic personalities are fairly well formed in the first seven years of life. Although it is a truth that most of us find ourselves reluctant to accept, it is quite obvious that we do retain for the rest of our lives the psychological traits that we developed by age seven. If we were quiet and predominantly inward at that age, the chances are that we are still quiet and inward. If we were boisterous extroverts at age seven, the chances are that others still have to bear with our boisterous extroversion.

Although it is difficult to accept, the psychological scars that we have acquired during these first seven years tend to remain with us in some way for life. Usually no very deep psychological problems originate after this age. However, our scars and the scar tissue may be aggravated or inflamed by circumstances occurring later in life. The rather common prejudice is that we are personally the masters of our fates and the captains of our souls. The truth of the matter is that we are very largely shaped by others, who, in an almost frightening way, hold our destiny in their hands. We are, each of us, the product of those who have loved us . . . or have refused to love us.

Our lives are shaped
by those who love us –

and by those
who refuse to love us.

## Anxiety

There are three basic emotional problems
with which all of us must, to some extent, live.
The first of these is called *anxiety*. Anxiety
may be described as *the irrational fear of an
unknown object*. We are not quite sure what
it is that is bothering us, but we are aware of
the uneasiness in our mind. We can recognize
the effects of this uneasiness in our nervous
system and digestive tract. To the extent that
we bear the scar tissue of anxiety, we fear that
something is wrong or will go wrong. The
deeply anxious person lives under the menace
of Murphy's Law: "What can go wrong will
go wrong." Murphy's Law is illustrated each
time that we drop our toast. It always lands
jam-side down.

The defense mechanisms built into human
nature are many and complicated. Human
nature seems to seek its own merciful
anesthetics. For example, when we are enduring such great physical pain that the threshold
(endurance capacity) of pain is crossed,
nature often seeks the anesthetic of uncon-
sciousness: we faint. Insanity itself is often
seen as a common refuge for those who find
life unbearable. It is an escape from the real

and too painful world with which the individual finds it impossible to cope.

So with anxiety, human nature has its own built-in defense. Nature tends to constrict the general uneasiness of anxiety into particular fears called *phobias*. A phobia can be defined as *an irrational fear of a known but unrealistic object.* Rather than submit to the constant uneasiness of anxiety, nature seeks to relieve us by constricting and restricting this general queasiness into particular fears. There are many people, for example, who look under their beds at night before retiring. They continue this nightly search even though they have found nothing but dust there for many years. There are others who cannot endure the cloister of a closed-in place (claustro-phobia). Others are unable to endure the possible perils of a high place (acrophobia). These phobias, which are designed to spare us from the constant tremors of anxiety, are usually deep-seated in the seriously anxious person.

Causes in the genesis of anxiety are not easy to trace. Psychologists, however, are becoming increasingly aware of the importance of what are called *prenatal experiences.* When a woman is carrying a child, the child is on its mother's bloodstream. Hematology (the study of blood and its diseases) has identified some of the changes in blood chemistry which occur during the traumatic moments of human life. We are all aware of the physical effects of our emotions. We experience adrenalin flushing into our bloodstream, a palpitating heart and the beads of perspiration that form on our forehead and in the palms of our hands.

The fetus or embryo, forming in its mother and nourished by her bloodstream, experiences these same impulses and effects. They are also transmitted by the muscular contractions of the mother's body, which the fetus likewise experiences. The preborn baby records these experiences and retains them both in its brain cells and nervous system, which is being formed during the period of gestation. When a woman is consistently upset emotionally during this period of pregnancy, the child to be born receives and retains the message of turbulence. It is transmitted via blood chemistry and muscular contraction. It is translated: This is a very insecure world into which you are coming.

We also know that the infant after birth is very sensitive to the hands that hold it. If it is dropped quickly or moved abruptly, this abrupt and unexpected motion causes an immediate nervous reaction. The infant will instinctively arch its back, and its muscles will stiffen. Only gradually will those muscles relax and become supple again. Infants do not hear soft sounds, but sudden, loud noises shock the infantile nervous system. Again the back will arch and stiffen, the muscles will become tense and rigid. Consequently, the nervous hands and abrupt movements, the exploding voices of the infant's parents will tend to reinforce the message of anxiety. And this message will be retained in the brain cells and nervous system of the child for life.

Very often we call the seriously anxious person a "worrywart." We tell these persons, in our naiveté and lack of compassion, that they shouldn't worry. We even accuse them of looking for things to worry about. Actually, the person who is given to worry has only indirect control over these instincts, and our lack of compassion is hardly of help to him or her.

# The Guilt Complex

The second basic emotional affliction, to which all of us are to some extent heirs, is called the *guilt complex*. The first thing that must be said about this guilt complex is that it does not have its origin in actual guilt. In fact, its origin is usually traceable to an age when serious, actual guilt would be impossible. A guilt complex may be described as *a haunting sense of personal moral evil or sinfulness*. The person who vividly experiences a guilt complex is constantly haunted by a deep personal feeling of sinfulness or evil. This complex often carries with it *a need to be punished*. Although it sounds rather bizarre, the person who is deeply afflicted by a sense of guilt will seek punishment unknowingly and unconsciously.

In its extreme manifestation, guilt may cause people to hurt themselves physically or to confess some crime of which they are not guilty. In a lesser but more common manifestation, guilt may cause people to seek a partner in marriage or the companionship of another who they somehow know will punish them. It is not uncommon for a person who has been married to, and suffered from, an alcoholic partner in marriage to remarry, after the demise of the first spouse, another alcoholic. In fact, there is a counterpart of Alcoholics Anonymous called Al-Anon for the families and relatives of active or recovering alcoholics. The emotional adjustments of living without punishment can, in some cases, be very great. This is not to say that all of the members of Al-Anon are the bearers of deep guilt complexes, but simply that this could be one of the emotional adjustments that must be made in the wake of alcoholic recovery.

As with anxiety, human nature has its own devices to lessen the suffering of the guilt complex. Just as anxiety tends to constrict itself into phobias, so the guilt complex tends to constrict itself into what are called *scruples*. The word *scruple* is derived from the Latin word, *scrupulum*. A *scrupulum* is a small pebble. When by accident a small pebble gets lodged inside one of our shoes, we feel intermittent stabs of pain as we walk along. So scrupulous persons, as they walk through life, feel the intermittent agonies of their imagined guilt. A scruple usually centers around some supposed sin or guilt. Just as the

phobia constricts and concretizes the generalized fear of anxiety, so does the scruple
constrict and concretize the generalized sense
of guilt. Consequently, these bouts with
scruples, precisely because they are intermittent, spare the deeply guilty person from the
generalized and constant agony of his or her
complex.

The origin of the guilt complex is usually
traceable to severe or harsh parents. Perhaps
such parents have rationalized that their
severity is designed to produce well-
disciplined children. They justify their outbursts of emotional rage and the ventilation
of their own personal discomfort under the
holy name of "child training." When these
outbursts become a pattern of parental
conduct, the children of such parents may
well bear the scars of the "training." For the
rest of their lives these children may have to
deal with guilt complexes.

Some years ago a woman named Ruth
Krause wrote a book called *A Hole Is to Dig.*
In this book she relates the answers of groups
of children asked to define many of the
common realities of life. "Arms," one child
wrote, "are to hug." "Puppies are to jump all

over you and lick your face." "A hole is to dig." The deeper intent of Miss Krause was to illustrate that children do not think as adults. Imagine, for example, an angry father leaning down over his small son. He has blood in his eyes and flames are snorting from his nostrils. In a terrifying voice he shouts, "You *bad* boy! You crossed the street, and I told you not to!" The frightened child obviously does not understand the dangers of crossing a street. He does not know, because he does not think in terms of cause and effect. He does not understand the perils of a small child crossing the street alone. He will, however, retain this message: he is *bad.* Margaret Mead, in her book *And Keep Your Powder Dry,* insists on the necessity of conveying to a child a sense of being loved even when he or she is being scolded or punished. Punishment in anger is almost always, if not always, a very dangerous thing.

## The Inferiority Complex

The third basic emotional affliction is called the *inferiority complex.* It is a *sense of inadequacy as a person.* People who feel deeply inferior, as we all do to some extent, may be aware of certain particular abilities. However, there is inside of them the gnawing parasite of their own inadequacy. They feel that they are unacceptable as a person. They feel that they have very little personal worth. As opposed to the victim of a guilt complex, the person afflicted with an inferiority complex will feel not so much a sense of moral evil but of worthlessness. The genesis of the inferiority complex is, like the other emotional scars that we bear, traceable to one's very early life. For example, parents treat a child as though he or she were their bag and baggage, and train the child to a constant state of surrender to the almighty parental will. Such treatment can easily sow the seeds of an inferiority complex.

Dr. Benjamin Spock feels that the rigid enforcement of eating times and habits, and the rigid regulation of the other biological functions of a child's body, can well upset the emotional balance of that child for the rest of his or her life. The message of inferiority is transmitted by mothers who do not wish to reheat food and fathers who will not tolerate a floor full of toys at any time because it is inconvenient to them. They are saying, by implication, "You have no worth of your own. Your whole good is to go along with us, and not to rock the boat of our convenience." This is not to issue an indictment against a reasonable and loving discipline of children. Obviously, children must learn that others have rights, and they must be trained to realize that they are to respect the convenience of others. However, when this training is exaggerated, children are led to believe that their whole worth is to respect the desires and convenience of their parents and elders. They will, then, instinctively conclude that they have no worth of themselves, a lesson that will sabotage their self-confidence, perhaps for life.

It should be noted that most of the effective lessons that children need in order to be prepared for life are taught by example rather than by angry or severe words. When we wish to teach a child how to blow up a balloon, we do not give a set of verbal instructions and expect the child to absorb them. A child is not so much a thinker as an imitator. So we blow up the balloon ourselves, allow the air to escape, and ask the child to do the same thing. Being such an instinctive imitator, he or she can do it almost at once. The parents

who disguise the love of their own convenience under the title "child training" are
teaching their child habits of self-centeredness
which can bring on only unhappiness. We
have said that the first seven years of life are
the critical years. Much of what is called the
*basic human option,* either to *love* (to seek
others and their happiness) or to *lust* (to seek
self and one's own gratification), will be
determined by the lessons of parental example
and the osmosis of childlike imitation.

# CHAPTER THREE

# The self-image

It is almost a truism in contemporary psychology that the self-image lies at the root of most human conduct. What is more difficult to accept is that the self-image that each of us has is really the product of what other people, rightly or wrongly, have told us that we are. If we imagine ourselves to be evil or inadequate, our life will be governed by Murphy's Law. Some form of self-destruction will show in our conduct. We will attempt nothing of challenge and will consider safety as that which must be sought above and before all. We will somehow attempt to hide our shame or inadequacy

*You better not compromise yourself. It's all you got.*

**JANIS JOPLIN**

under a veil of anonymity. The one thing we cannot do—and it is the one thing every human being must do to be fully alive—is accept ourselves as we are.

The whole theory of Dr. Carl Rogers, famous for his nondirective or client-centered system of counseling, is based on the need for self-acceptance. Dr. Rogers maintains that the basic challenge of every human life is that of self-understanding and self-acceptance. He further postulates that we cannot understand and accept ourselves as we are until someone else has first understood and accepted us for what we are. Finally, Rogers maintains that once we have been accepted as we are and loved for what we are, the symptomatic problems with which most of us struggle in life will yield to this self-knowledge and self-acceptance.

Consequently, Rogers suggests that the role of a counselor (and this might well be applied to the role of a friend) is largely to listen as the client describes his or her problems and ultimately himself or herself. The counselor must convey a sense of acceptance to the counselee, without yielding to the impulse of saddling him or her with gems of advice and direction. To be successful at this type of counseling or friendship, one must make an act of faith that our great human need is to know and accept ourselves as we are. We are too often tempted to think that putting others in their place, or taking them down a peg, or forcing them to face reality is the pathway to solution. In fact, harsh criticism that hits at the person rather than the deed only deepens the problem because it makes self-acceptance more difficult.

Dr. Maxwell Maltz, a plastic surgeon, discovered that when his surgical arts had removed some physical ugliness or helped to achieve a more pleasing physical appearance, patients frequently underwent a transformation of personality. They became more confident, more outgoing, and exhibited a newly emancipated human spirit. In pursuing his investigation of this phenomenon, the surgeon turned to the inner image, as opposed to the external physical appearance, and discovered that this inner self-image controls so much of human conduct and happiness. In his book *Psycho-Cybernetics,* Dr. Maltz depicts the ugly self-image as the radical cause of most human inertia, failure, and unhappiness.

The importance of one's self-image is aptly illustrated in the fairy tale "Rapunzel." It is the story of a young girl, imprisoned in a tower with an old witch. The young girl is in fact very beautiful, but the old witch insistently tells her that she is ugly. It is, of course, a strategem of the witch to keep the girl in the tower with herself. The moment of Rapunzel's liberation occurs one day when she is gazing from the window of the tower. At the base of the tower stands her Prince Charming. She throws her hair, long and beautiful golden tresses, out the window (the root ends, of course, remain attached to her head), and he braids the hair into a ladder and climbs up to rescue her. Rapunzel's imprisonment is really not that of the tower but the fear of her own ugliness which the witch has described so often and so effectively. However, when Rapunzel sees in the mirroring eyes of her Prince Charming that she is beautiful, she is freed from the real tyranny of her own imagined ugliness.

This is true not only in the case of Rapunzel but with all of us. We desperately need to see in the mirror of another's eyes our own goodness and beauty, if we are to be truly free. Until this moment, we, too, will remain

locked inside the prison towers of ourselves.
The thrust of love requires us to be outside
of ourselves and to be preoccupied with the
happiness and fulfillment of others. Consequently, we will not love very much until we
have had this vision of our own goodness and
giftedness.

## Ego-defense Mechanisms

We have already mentioned that human
nature is resourceful in the matter of self-
defense. This resourcefulness is perhaps
nowhere better illustrated than in the ego-
defense mechanisms that we employ to
protect ourselves from the chimeras of
anxiety, guilt, and inferiority complexes.
Rather than expose a self that we imagine to
be inadequate or ugly, we instinctively build
walls of isolation. This, of course, is contrary
to Robert Frost's advice: Do not build a wall
until you know what you are walling in and
what you are walling out. To the extent that
we experience scars of anxiety, guilt, and
inferiority feelings, we are tempted to wear
masks, to act out roles. We do not trust or
accept ourselves enough to be ourselves.
These walls and masks are measures of

NEVER BUILD A WALL
UNTIL YOU KNOW
WHAT YOU'RE WALLING IN—
AND WHAT YOU'RE
WALLING OUT.

self-defense, and we will live behind our walls and wear our masks as long as they are needed.

While it may seem to be a safer life behind these facades, it is also a lonely life. We cease to be authentic, and as persons we starve to death. The deepest sadness of the mask is, however, that we have cut ourselves off from all genuine and authentic contact with the real world and with other human beings. We must remember that this world and these human beings hold our potential maturity and fulfillment in their hands. We must interact honestly with them. When we resort to acting out roles or wearing masks, there is no possibility of human and personal growth. We are simply not being ourselves, and we cannot emerge as persons without an atmosphere of growth. We are merely performing on a stage. When the curtain drops after our performance, we will remain the same immature persons that we were when the curtain went up at the beginning of the act.

Very often our masks are obviously pretentious or ugly. The small boy walking through the dark cemetery in the dead of night whistles to convince himself and others who may be with him that he is not afraid. We call it "whistling in the dark." We know that the small boy who dreams of becoming a basketball star walks on the tips of his toes, trying to be something that he fears he isn't. More obnoxious perhaps are the people who bite their nails inwardly but wear the pretentious mask of arrogance on the outside. Eventually the public, which sits in attendance on such an act, sees through it.

There is a strong human temptation to judge people only in terms of their acts or masks. It is all too rare that we are able to see through the sham and pretense of masks and find the insecure or wounded heart that is being camouflaged and is trying to protect itself from further injury. Consequently, we often lash out with the iron fists of criticism and sarcasm or we try to tear off the masks in exasperated anger. We fail to realize that masks are worn only as long as they are needed. Only the reassurance of an accepting and understanding love will lure the anxious, the guilt-ridden, and the supposedly inferior persons out from behind their defenses. It may well be that we ourselves are hiding behind such masks and walls, resulting in very

little human encounter and communication
. . . only mask facing mask, wall facing wall.

Generally, we can recognize masks. We
have a sense that someone is not authentic,
is pretentious, and we call that person a sham.
We very much dislike the mask of sarcasm,
and we resent the silent mask of the sphinx.
We try to sabotage the complacent mask of
cockiness in the young and the mask of
arrogance in the old. We do not realize that
in the unexposed roots of these exteriors,
there is only a cry of pain. There is the need
to be understood and loved into life. Most
of the obnoxious qualities that we find in
others are the result of some kind of defensive
convergence on self. Of course, we openly
resent this self-centered posture. It is then
that we must remember the psychiatrist's
question: "Did you ever have a toothache?"
We must learn to look through the sham and
pretense of our fellow human beings, to
alleviate the pain and the lonely voids that
have constructed these walls of defense.
Direct attacks on these defenses will only
result in their reinforcement.

The main
thing
in life
is
not to be
afraid
to be
human.

PABLO CASALS

# The Subconscious Mind

Psychologists tell us of two levels of the human mind: the *conscious* and the *subconscious*. It is obvious from the terminology itself that we are conscious or aware of the contents of our conscious minds; we are unaware of the contents of the subconscious level of our minds. Consequently, it is sometimes called the "unconscious." These two levels of the mind have been compared to the upstairs and downstairs of a human dwelling. When we find eyesores, a worn-out piece of furniture or an unsightly pail of garbage, we instinctively want to put them out of our sight—into the basement. There we will not have to look at them. So it is with the two levels of the mind. When we cannot face or live with some reality or attitude that we find in ourselves, we can bury this reality or attitude into our subconscious minds. When we wish to forget some *event* of our lives, and deliberately hide it in the confines of the subconscious, this is called *suppression*. When we discover in ourselves some *attitude* or *emotional reaction* that we consider unworthy, we often put it out of sight and into the subconscious mind. This is called *repression*.

Eventually, when the subconscious mind becomes overloaded, we find ourselves very uncomfortable. We are unaware of the exact source of our discomfort, precisely because the real conflict has been buried in our subconscious. What we bury there is not buried dead but alive, and remains alive. Sometimes we try to find an antagonism of the present moment upon which to lay the blame for our discomforts, but the roots of our pain can be found only in the subconscious mind.

For example, when children are not loved and not given a sense of their own personal worth by their parents, they will tend to react in one of two ways: they will take the path of either external conformity or external rebellion. But there will always be resentment because they have been deprived of their psychological needs. However, society and our culture will not allow us to express this resentment, real as it may be. When a child tries to express this resentment to his or her parents, they often remind the child forcibly that they are his or her parents and deserve to be loved. The fact of the matter is that they may not be very lovable. And so their insistent demand to be loved will place the

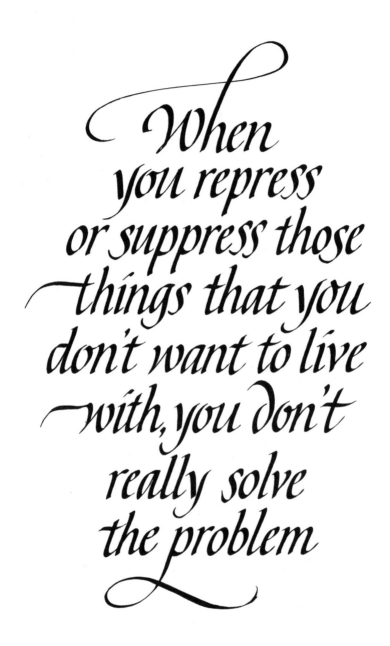

When
you repress
or suppress those
things that you
don't want to live
with, you don't
really solve
the problem

because
you don't bury
the problem dead—
you bury it alive.
It remains alive
and active
inside of
you.

child in a position of deep emotional conflict.
Parents who are adamant in their insistence
that their children obey the fourth commandment to honor father and mother should
make an equal effort to be honorable.

Children in whom inevitable resentment is
growing usually cannot express this resentment. They are made to feel that it is a very
evil thing. Should they try to express this to
others outside their family, they may well be
called an "ingrate" and made to feel ashamed
for having such an attitude toward their
parents.

The stage has now been set for repression.
Not knowing what to do with their resentment, children will hide it in the basement of
their mind. It is like a splinter of wood that
has been pushed deeply under the flesh,
where it will fester and cause agony. The
resentment in children who are not ade-
quately loved will be a source of much
long-lasting pain. There is always the chance
that this resentment, gathering too much
force in the subconscious mind, may boil
over into acts of violence or vandalism. The
wrong people may have to bear the brunt of
this hidden or repressed resentment.

As another example, a very common repression is the repressed need for affection and love. Very often in our culture such needs cannot be acknowledged or expressed. They do not coincide with the image of independence and self-sufficiency that is thrust upon us by our society and culture. Consequently, people who have these repressed needs will have to seek gratification of these needs in devious and subtle ways. Most of the time these people are deceiving themselves as well as others.

It has been said that liquor, in releasing inhibitions, often opens the door to the repressions in the subconscious. The woman who becomes argumentative and antagonistic under the mild influence of liquor is probably releasing her repressed hostilities. The man who wants to put his arms around everyone in the place, male or female, may be releasing something of his repressed needs to be loved. We will recall that in T. S. Eliot's play *The Cocktail Party,* the author portrays a man under the influence of liquor leaning over to a psychiatrist at the Cocktail Party. He pleads with the psychiatrist for this favor: Please make me feel important.

And this is what *psychoanalysis* is all about. The analyst dredges the contents of the subconscious mind. He or she helps clients realize what their problems really are, and tries to help them solve or live with their problems.

Although hypnosis and narcotherapy (the use of truth serums) are sometimes used in psychoanalysis, the most common technique is called *free association*. Clients are helped by the analyst to associate their present thoughts with memories of their past. Gradually they learn to link what they feel in the here and now to the historical and radical causes of these feelings. The analyst may also attempt to interpret clients' dreams, the matter for which is supplied largely by the subconscious mind since the conscious mind (being asleep) is not active during sleep.

Needless to say, the process of psycho-analysis should be left to those who are professionally competent. The only point in bringing this up is to illustrate the reality of the subconscious mind and the fact that we often do not understand our own motivation and the root causes of our own discomfort.

# Transference

Very often we are strongly impelled by the
needs that we have buried in the subconscious. The need to be loved, to feel
important, and to accept self can very often,
even when we are unaware of it, have a
profound influence on our conduct and
dealings with others. *Transference,* in the
sense that we are here using it (it does have
another usage), is always *a subconscious
process by which we "transfer" our needs to
others.* For example, if we wish to feel
important, we may seek to lord it over others,
to dominate them. If we were to be asked
about such conduct, we would heartily and
stubbornly maintain that this is the way that
others need to be treated. It is for their own
good. Actually, we may be transferring our
own subconscious need to them. A young
person may well enter upon an occupation
of notable altruism on the grounds that he
or she wishes to make a contribution to a
needy world. While this may in fact be the
case, it may also be that subconsciously this
person has an unsatisfied need to be needed.

Very often mothers or fathers are overprotective of their children, on the alleged

grounds that they wish no harm to come to them. They may well be subconsciously transferring their own need to have their children remain dependent upon them. They do not want them to grow up. It is good for us to be aware of this possibility of transfer-ence in our lives, to be aware that we may well be seeking ourselves under the guise of altruism and love. Still, there is really no way to lay open all the intricacies of human motivation or to explore all our own subcon-scious needs. The only effective measures that we can take are to renew our motivation and to locate the focus of the mind on those we are trying to serve and help. If we can consistently do this, we will gradually acquire the habit that is called love.

## The Need for Professional Help

Our age has sometimes been called "the age of the couch." Sometimes we interpret the presence of stress and strain in our lives and inside of ourselves as an indication of the need for professional psychological or psychi-atric help. The stigma of seeking such professional help has largely been removed in these times. Perhaps this is due to the admission of many movie stars and national heroes that they have sought and been helped by such professional treatment. However, suppression, repression, subconscious needs, and transference are a part of the psychological makeup of all of us. Hopefully, we will seek such professional help if and when we need it.

We have mentioned at the beginning of this book the dynamics of human personality and the possibility that these dynamics can become impeded. If they are impeded to such an extent that people are able to neither experience true, meaningful human friendship nor perform in reasonable proportion to their capacities, there is then indication that they need professional help.

A true and meaningful human friendship supposes more than mere association with another. It supposes that we are able to share ourselves, to reveal ourselves to another who is our friend. It supposes that we can entrust our friend with our secrets and accept his or her confidences. It is the human relationship that Martin Buber calls the "I-Thou" encounter.

There is always some gap between our absolute potential and actual performance.

Love is
essentially
a relationship.

We never fully realize our absolute potential
nor translate perfectly our best intentions into
external accomplishments. Yet, when there is
a considerable gap between potential and
performance, as when students of considerable intellectual endowment cannot pass
their courses in school or when competent
workers cannot perform sufficiently to hold
a job for a very long time, there is some
indication that the dynamics of personality
have been seriously jammed. In such cases
there is need of professional assistance.

A further indication of this need may arise
from what are called *psychosomatic illnesses.*
Because of the mysterious but very real
interrelation of soul and body, the buried
disturbances of the mind may express themselves in physical reactions. However, this
should be left to the professional judgment
of a competent physician. And finally, prolonged *depression,* which indicates the presence of some disturbance, can be an indication that a person is in need of professional
help. There are times, of course, when we all
feel depressed. The depression that is symptomatic of a deeper problem is usually a
crippling and prolonged depression. But again
it will be expressed in the inability of the

person involved to accomplish a meaningful
friendship and to perform in reasonable
proportion to his or her ability.

## The Need for Friendship

While the person in need of professional help
should seek out competent and professional
assistance, all of us have the need for the
"supportive psychotherapy" of friendship.
We are, each of us, a conglomeration of
mysterious needs and impulses which need
to be expressed. We need to be able to express
ourselves, to talk ourselves out without fear
of rejection by others. Too often the problems that we keep submerged within us
remain, in the darkness of our own interior,
undefined and therefore destructive. We are
as sick as we are secretive. We do not see the
true dimensions of these things that trouble
us until we define them and set lines of
demarcation in conversation with a friend.
Inside us they remain as nebulous as smoke.
But when we confide ourselves to another,
we acquire some sense of dimension and
objectivity. And this enables growth in
self-identity and the capacity to accept ourselves as we really are.

It may well be that our walls and masks will make this difficult. We may instinctively try to rationalize that there is really no one near to whom we can talk ourselves out. Many of us practice the self-deception of believing that there is no one in our supposed circle of friends who can be trusted. Very commonly these excuses that we have constantly rehearsed are merely excuses. Our real fear is that we would be rejected. We fear that the other person would not understand us. And so we wait and wait and wait behind our walls for the sufficient sound of reassurance in another, or we gaze out of the windows of our towers, looking for a Prince Charming to come and rescue us. We excuse ourselves from all initiative in seeking a truly human, interpersonal relationship on the grounds that the time is not ripe or the circumstances right. In the meanwhile, we can only perish. We will very likely "act out" the problems that remain submerged within us if we refuse to "talk out" these problems. We will act out our hostilities by destructively criticizing those around us. We will act out our need to be loved by an emotional overdependence upon others. We will act out our repressed sense of inferiority by trying to humiliate others or dominate them.

It is so much wiser to take all the risks of confiding in another than to live alone behind walls and masks, blindly acting out the things that we refuse to talk out. And we must remember, if we want to love others truly, that these repressed and suppressed problems are very definitely impediments to love. They are our toothaches which keep us converged on ourselves. They keep us from being ourselves, and keep us from forgetting ourselves.

# CHAPTER FOUR

# The maturing process

We speak of people as being mature or
immature. However, the fact is that all of
human life should represent an ever-
continuing growth toward full maturity.
What we have called the dynamics of human
personality are very much involved in this process of self-revelation and of self-expansion.
Consequently, almost all the signs of im-
maturity are somehow characterized by a
convergence upon self. This self-centeredness
betrays itself in many ways: bearing grudges
and prejudices, pouting, emotionalized
thinking, exaggerated feelings of inferiority,
overconcern about the opinions that

# Becoming is superior to being.

Paul Klee

others have of us, worrying, overdependence upon parents or family, rebellious and angry attitudes, bragging or bullying, temper tantrums, the negativism of destructive criticism, procrastination, self-indulgence, "slapstick" humor which is humiliating to another, flirtations, and so on.

The patterns of maturity, on the other hand, are recognized in the following: going out to others, getting along with them, exercising a reasonable self-sufficiency, setting realistic goals, exercising discretion, differentiating the important and unimportant things in life, demonstrating flexibility, adaptability, and emotional stability.

We might divide human maturity into four parts. *Intellectual maturity* is characterized by the ability to form one's own opinion while respecting but not leaning on the opinions of others, and the ability to make one's own decisions, with all due respect to substantial evidence and the counsel of others, independently and firmly. Intellectually mature people are willing to change their minds in the light of new and important evidence and to modify their plans if such seems to be wise. They have their own thoughts. They make their own decisions and accept full responsibility for them. They are willing to accept responsibilities and to acknowledge the truth even when it is displeasing or makes serious demands of them. They do not approach their problems by worrying over them. They analyze each problem, consider the alternatives, make a decision, execute and live with that decision.

*Emotional maturity* is characterized by the acceptance of emotions together with the ability to keep them under reasonable control. Emotionally mature people can live with emotionally demanding situations without falling apart. They learn to deal with these situations objectively. They talk out grievances rather than pout; they can accept criticism without feeling deeply hurt; they can face and do unpleasant things without running away from them; they are not overcome by unrealistic fears and anxieties. Both the radical, who wants to change everything from the ground up, and the reactionary, who does not want anyone to rock the boat and who is deeply devoted to the *status quo,* are emotionally immature. This has been pointed out by Martin Peck in his book *The Meaning of Psychoanalysis.*

Both radicals and reactionaries represent an unresolved attitude toward domineering parental authority, long after the reality of the situation has ceased to exist. Radicals have sought to rebel and have never outgrown this rebellious attitude. Reactionaries have chosen to conform and for their own security will probably tend to be conformists all of their lives. They will fear to attempt new accomplishments on their own, and they will be reluctant to accept whatever is new.

*Social maturity* is characterized by the ability to go out to others, to relate well with them, and to accomplish meaningful friendships. Socially mature people are not too dependent on their own families or friends, nor do they wage war with them. They can adjust themselves to the laws and conventions of the society in which they live, and they are able to subordinate themselves to the achievement of group ideals and the fulfillment of group needs. They find that work can be interesting, in spite of its unpleasant and humdrum aspects.

*Moral maturity* is characterized by the devotion to moral ideals and the ability to live them out. Children's morals are generally instinctual and unreasoned. They are the morals of their parents and those around them. In adolescence, morally maturing people will conceive their own ideals and will have a fairly definite and intelligent method of arriving at them. With ever-deepening maturity, a person's ideals usually become more realistic and consistent, and at the same time firmer. In general, it can be said that morally mature people have come to their ideals in a perspective that is worldwide rather than egocentric.

Since maturity is an ever-evolving process and progress, it can be marked by halts *(fixations)* and recessions *(regressions)*. There are in each of us two conflicting tendencies: to grow up and to turn back. In general when life demands more of us than we feel capable of giving, we develop what has been called "promotional neurosis." We have difficulty in adjusting to increased responsibilities. So we tend to back away from them.

H. Crichton Miller in his book *The New Psychology and the Teacher* suggests that the two most common causes of fixation and/or regression are:

Most adults
never
grow up.

1. domineering parental authority
2. a too harsh presentation of reality

Domineering parental authority stifles individuality and self-expression; people can mature only to the extent that they are allowed to be themselves. Each is a unique person and must be allowed to be and express what he or she is. A presentation of reality which seems too harsh is puzzling to children and becomes too much for their powers of adjustment; and so they do not follow their predominantly biological urge to grow up. Rather, they fixate or regress to escape the challenge.

*Fixation* represents an arrested emotional development. It is usually a case of apron strings, ''smother love,'' and excessive dependence on the thoughts and decisions of others. *Regression* is a returning to a lower stage of development; it is living in the past.

> *Backward, turn backward, O Time,*
> *In your flight.*
> *Make me a child again, just*
> *For tonight.*
>
> Elizabeth Akers Allen

It is the ''Old Oaken Bucket Complex'' (cf. poem by William Wordsworth):

*How dear to this heart are the*
*Scenes of my childhood,*
*When fond recollection presents them*
  *to view.*

Memory often distorts the possibilities of the
past, and glamorizes what might have been
(cf. Wendell White, *The Psychology of*
*Dealing with People,* p. 75). Regression is
well illustrated in the so-called "grown-ups"
who delight in the college reunion or business
convention so they can act like a "kid" again.

Regression is usually a return to a point of
previous fixation. For example, the devoted
daughter, who was the little darling of her
parents, may be impelled to run home to them
when her marriage becomes difficult. She may
want to regress to the stage or point of
fixation when she was a little darling. She
refuses to accept the challenge of being a
grown-up mother and wife. The dominant
motive for such regression, as we have said,
is usually the reluctance to accept new
challenges and responsibilities.

Children who have been pampered (and
this applies chiefly to the ages of three to
twelve), who have been given everything and
asked nothing, are often predisposed to

regress later in life to cantankerous and childish bids for attention. Frustrations and anger, also, if carried inside of a person too long without release in conversation with another, tend to result in regression.

## Maturation and Needs

*Infancy* is the period covering the first two years of life. We must recall what we have said about anxiety and its transmission during infancy. Here the stress must be placed on the positive needs of children at this stage. The chief need of infants is for tender love, which is communicated primarily through the sense of touch. If infants are shown much love and given the sense that they are lovable during this period, they will grow up to expect friendliness from others and be more dis-posed to love others for themselves. It should be remarked that infancy is the time of a human being's first impression of life. In general, it is necessary that this first impres-sion be one of security, tenderness, and love. Infancy is not the stage in which children can be "spoiled."

*Childhood* embraces the third to the twelfth year of life. It is during this period that children begin to establish their own individuality and self-esteem. Parents must guard against the two extremes of overprotection and rejection. Children who are overprotected, for whom parents do everything and whose every activity is supervised with watchful parental eyes, are never taught the self-reliance that is a part of growing up. They are not being prepared to accept hardships. They are not being trained to make responsible decisions.

The greatest accomplishment during the period of childhood is training in socialization. A child must be taught to share and cooperate, to relinquish the self-centered world of the infant. About the age of three, children try to grow into relationships with others; and at the same time they are busy trying to become unique individuals. When they become frustrated or disoriented by this double effort, children come into what is known as "the age of resistance." They resort to hostile refusals. They may try to return to being a baby again, or introvertedly to turn away from reality. They may try to console themselves with thumb sucking; or they might exhibit spiteful rebellion, resist feeding, and stage temper tantrums. However, by age five children usually recover and have developed a clearer concept of their own personal status and the wisdom of adult authority.

The most critical problem in childhood is that of *discipline*. The central directive is this: give as few commands as are strictly required and then see that they are carried out. To give too many commands will justifiably seem unreasonable to children and they will rebel. During this period, parental discipline should gradually yield to self-discipline. Only by practice can children develop self-reliance and a sense of personal responsibility.

A second very serious problem that often occurs in this stage is that of *jealousy*. Older children should be given some time exclusively for themselves and some explanation that the new baby has more needs, that it is more helpless, and so on. Otherwise the jealousy of the older children can lead to anger and even hatred of their parents. There might also rise up in them feelings of failure and shame and possibly a lasting resentment for the younger child who is the object of their jealousy. Usually this jealousy can be forestalled by giving older children rights of seniority, by encouraging them to help with the care of the baby, and by consistently reminding them of their own unique personal worth.

*Adolescence* is the period that extends by definition from age twelve to twenty-one. Adolescence has been called the period of "storms and stress." Our American-type civilization creates much of this strain, storm, and stress by its own pressures and choices. For example, young people in our culture must decide about going to college, accepting political affiliation, achieving self-support, choosing a profession, and establishing whole-some relationships with the opposite sex.

In our American culture parents often unknowingly use certain ploys that deepen the storm and stress of adolescence. For example, they may deprive the young of emotional security by offering or withdrawing signs of affection as a source of coercion. So many parents offer signs of love only on the condition of surrender to their will and whims. Likewise, many parents goad their children into a relentless pursuit of success by implicitly threatening to withdraw their love in case of failure. This threat of rejection subjects children to serious emotional strain;

it makes them feel that they must be good or smart, and so on. In general, children can endure serious emotional strain from other sources if the tender and loving care of their parents is present.

The main conflict in adolescents is between two tendencies: *gregariousness* and *individuation.* Adolescents seek to be accepted by others (gregariousness) and at the same time they want to be themselves (individuation). Conformity appears to be the price of popularity, and yet it asks the submission of individuality. Adolescents who make this submission slavishly do not build up a sense of who and what they really are, and are consequently confused. Conformity to the peer group and the acceptance of the many status symbols of adolescent society can tend to imprison young men or women just when they are seeking to be free and to be themselves. The more acceptance adolescents receive in their own home and from their own family, the less they will be subjected to peer pressure and the less they will be inclined to conform to the arbitrary standards of their peers.

The tension is concretely between social acceptance and the denial of individuality.

The real problem is not
that God is dead
but that
we are supposed to
reflect God and to stand
as symbols of God,
especially for the young.
God is dead in us —
because we have never
understood God.

Adolescents are torn between the achievement of personal confidence and underlying uncertainty. They sincerely question answers given them, yet they can appear very sure of themselves. This sureness is very often only a compensatory cover or mask for their uncertainty. The doubts they have are encouraging symptoms of intellectual awakening. Adolescents question authority and even their religious faith. They are trying to make their convictions their own. They must never be scolded for this. It is the time of life when they most need the sensitive sympathy and tolerance of their parents.

Adolescents are especially sensitive to criticism and disparagement. They need abundant affection, encouragement, praise, and attention to counteract the demoralizing experiences of the classroom, the competition on the athletic field, and the scramble for social acceptance. Bragging or belittling others is only their way to conceal personal insecurity, and its importance should not be exaggerated. Those who volunteer to "take them down a peg" do them a great disservice.

The most serious adjustment of adolescents is the emancipation from family bonds.

Overprotective or possessive parents are terribly frustrating to them, and they may develop an allergy for all authority as a result. They may even try to appear to be dirty or disheveled to serve notice to the world that all parental training in cleanliness has been successfully rejected. The emancipation that should be taking place during this time involves "a gradual emergence from parental supervision. Young people seek reliance upon the security that they can give themselves rather than upon the security provided by parents. They must be helped to develop an attitude toward parents as friends rather than as protectors or supervisors. Young people must be educated in the planning of their own time and in the making of their own decisions, without overbearing parental control" (adapted from Luella Cole, *The Psychology of Adolescence,* 3rd edition, p. 7).

The problem of sexual urges is a very real source of confusion to adolescents. If they are to learn the true relationship between sex and love, it is important that they feel free to discuss these matters with their parents— openly and without shame. They must be helped to accept their new sexual feelings as normal, natural, and good. They must also learn the wisdom of self-control. Sexual indulgence is very commonly a sign of regression to primitive and infantile forms of satisfaction and gratification. Maturity in this matter of sexuality will generally bring with it a total maturation; failure to grow in this area usually results in fixations or regression. Sexual indulgence does not afford a much needed feeling of security, nor will it satisfy affectional and emotional needs. If, however, the affectional and emotional needs of adolescence are satisfied in controlled relationships with members of the opposite sex and within their own family, the sexual urge will be far easier for adolescents to control. Masturbation and other efforts at sexual self-gratification are usually symptomatic of fixation or regression in personal development. Such indulgence educates the deepest human neuro-vegetative instincts primarily to seek personal gratification. Unless these instincts are correctly educated in adolescence, there will be a deep and permanent stamp of selfishness on the person at the instinctual level. This will present a serious, if not insuperable, obstacle to the ability to grow in love.

Most men lead lives
of quiet desperation.

Thoreau

## Positive vs. Negative Reinforcements of the Will

Sometimes we speak of the will as though it were a muscle, either strong or weak. This manner of speaking can easily obscure a very important reality about human conduct. The will is not itself weak or strong in us; it is rather our *motivation* that is weak or strong. It is also important to realize that *reasons* for good conduct are not the same as *motives*. We might well enumerate many good reasons for doing this or that, but they are not motives unless they move us. The Latin word *movere* means "to move," and it is this word from which our word *motive* is derived.

Because, as we said in the beginning, every person is unique, it is also true that what will move one person might well leave another unmoved. If a good reason is to become a motive for the will, its goodness must be somehow exposed and made attractive to the person in question. The imposition of authority cannot, in itself, produce virtue; it may well produce conformity, but conformity is not always virtue. Virtue must come from within a person. It must be the product of an interior act of the will seeking a good, and the will responds only to motives whose good is recognized.

Psychologists, in studying human motivation, have found that *positive* reinforcements of the will (rewards for good conduct) are infinitely more effective than *negative* reinforcements (punishments for bad conduct). To be constantly critical of young people is obviously a dangerous thing. It tends to undermine their confidence and to make all authority obnoxious. However, if we take the approach of positive reinforcements, we tend to overlook small failures in conduct but never fail to recognize and reward (at least with a kind word) the desired conduct. The effect will be almost magical. It is a further illustration of the power released in the creation of a good self-image. Most people will be in their conduct what we tell them they are.

If we build pedestals, young people will climb up on them. However, if we keep our hands on the edge of the rug, always ready to pull it out from under them, there can only be trouble ahead.

# Learning to love

The whole process of maturation depends on *how we react* to the difficulties or challenges of life. Immature people see only the difficulties. They pay very little attention to their own reactions, which are, in fact, the critical and definitive thing. Difficulties pass, but our reaction to them does not. As William James has suggested, there may be a God in heaven who forgives us our sins, but human nature does not. Our failures are memorized in our mind, muscles, fibers, and brain cells. Each reaction, mature or immature, lingers on in us as the beginning of a habit. Repeated mature reactions tend to

produce the formed habits of maturity.
Eventually they define us. Repeated immature
reactions dig their own destructive grooves.

Christians must always accept themselves
in their present human condition, which will
inevitably involve failure. Ideals must always
be introduced to the test of actual experience.
This test of our ideals, which very often
sounds beautiful, can often become a struggle,
a renunciation, a battle for control of self, a
willingness to start again in the wake of
failures. It can involve a lucid acceptance of
the mystery of the cross.

It is not the problem—and in this case not
the isolated *failure*—that is critical, definitive,
and paramount. It is our *reaction to it.* The
reaction of Christians must always be suf-
fused with confidence. They should be
nourished by the conviction that with God
they are a majority, even stronger than their
own weakness. The process of maturation as
Christians and as human beings will inevitably
be marked by failures, but the only real failure
is to quit. When the situation gets tough,
Christians must get tougher. They must
become bigger than their problems. In the
end, such determination to love will bring

unless
you love someone
nothing else
makes any sense.

e.e. cummings

them to the feet of love itself, which is their
eternal victory in the victorious Christ.

## The Paradox of Love

All of us experience at some time or another
a feeling of loneliness and isolation. From
time to time we experience a very painful void
inside ourselves that becomes an unbearable
prison. We have all felt at some time alienated
from others, separated from the group, alone
and lonely. By its very nature this loneliness,
like all of our toothaches, centers the focus
of attention on ourselves. We seek to fill this
void, to satisfy this hunger . . . we go out to
find others who will love us.

We may do things for them in an obvious
attempt to gain their love. We may come to
them with hands stretched out like pan scales.
On the one hand is our donation to them, the
other hand being extended to receive their
donation to us. We may even be deceived
into thinking that this exchange is loving.

We know that our loneliness can be filled
only by the love of others. We know that we
must feel loved. The paradox is this: if we try
to fill the void of our own loneliness by
seeking love from others, we will inevitably

find no consolation but only a deeper desolation. It is true that "You're Nobody Till Somebody Loves You." Only the person who has experienced love is capable of growing. It is a frightening but true reality of human life that by loving me or refusing to love me, others hold the potential of my maturity in their hands. Most of us, driven by our own aching needs and voids, turn to life and other people in the stance of seekers. We become what C. S. Lewis, in his book *The Four Loves,* calls "those pathetic people who simply want friends and can never make any. The very condition of having friends is that we should want something else besides friends." Most of us know our need to be loved and try to seek the love that we need from others. But the paradox remains uncompromised: if we *seek* the love which we need, we will *never find it.* We are lost.

Love can effect the solution of our problems, but we must face the fact that to be loved, we must become lovable. When people orient their lives toward the satisfaction of their own needs, when they go out to seek the love that they need, no matter how we try to soften our judgments of them, they are self-centered. They are not lovable, even if they do deserve our compassion. They are concentrating on themselves, and as long as they continue to concentrate on themselves, their ability to love will always remain stunted and they will remain seriously immature.

If, however, people seek not to receive love, but rather to give it, they will become lovable and they will most certainly be loved in the end. This is the immutable law under which we live: concern for self and convergence upon self can only isolate self and induce an even deeper and more torturous loneliness. It is a vicious and terrible cycle that closes in on us when loneliness, seeking to be relieved through the love of others, only grows deeper.

The only way we can break this cycle formed by our aching egos is *to stop being concerned with ourselves* and *to begin to be concerned with others.* This, of course, is not easy. To relocate the focus of our minds from self to others can, in fact, require a lifetime of effort and work. It is made more difficult because we must put others in the forefront, in place of ourselves. We must learn to respond to the needs of others without seeking the satisfaction of our own needs.

There is such a thing
as a peace-of-soul approach
to religion.
It makes of God
a gigantic Bayer aspirin...

take God three times a day
and you won't feel any pain.

In his book *Religion and Personality,*
psychologist-priest Adrian van Kaam insists
that if we seek our own happiness and
fulfillment, we will never find them. However, if we do find our own happiness and
fulfillment, it will be because we have
forgotten ourselves and have sought the
happiness and fulfillment of those around us.
The problem is that most of us are clutching
to our own life rafts. We are tempted to
preoccupation with our own self-fulfillment.
Everything we do is somehow designed to
achieve our own safety and happiness. We
can be selfish in very refined and subtle ways.
Such preoccupation with self is an absolute
obstacle to human happiness and fulfillment,
because human happiness and fulfillment can
be attained only through genuine love. Each
of us must make a basic decision about how
we intend to spend our lives. If we decide to
spend our lives in the pursuit of our own
happiness and fulfillment, we are destined to
failure and desolation. If we decide to spend
our lives seeking the fulfillment and happiness
of others, and this is what is implied in love,
we shall certainly attain our own happiness
and fulfillment.

People who want only their own fulfillment, or who decide to love in order to be
fulfilled, will find that their love is in vain
because the focus remains on themselves.
People can grow only as much as their horizon
allows. Those who decide to love in order to
be fulfilled and happy will be disappointed
and will not grow because the horizon is still
constricted to themselves. Consequently, we
cannot conceive of love in any way as a means
of self-fulfillment, because if we do, we will
still be locked into the treacherous vicious
circle. We will be traveling always from our
own needs through others and back into
ourselves. We can never use others simply as
means to our satisfactions. They must always
be the end object of love. We will attain
maturity only in proportion to the shifting
of the focus of our minds away from ourselves and our own needs and away from the
self-centered desire to satisfy those needs.

Loving others can be truly accomplished
only when the focus of our minds and the
object of our desires is another. When we
love, all of our activity results from concern
for another and not from concern for
ourselves. We have said that if people truly

love in this way, they will be loved and they must be open to accept and enjoy the love of others. However, the delusion to be avoided at all costs is to love in order to receive love in return. I must, as Jesus suggests, lose my life before I can gain it. I must find out that the only real receiving is in giving. I have to lose sight of my own life, and I cannot lose it if I always have it clearly before my own mind.

In other words, love means a concern for, acceptance of, and an interest in the others around me whom I am trying to love. It is a self-donation which may prove to be an altar of sacrifice. I can love others only to the extent that they are truly the focus of my mind, heart, and life. I can find myself only by forgetting myself. Love is indeed costly and challenging. Because of the inward pains that all of us bear and the scar tissues that are part of our human inheritance, learning to love can be difficult. Because of the competition and example of a self-grasping world, it is likewise difficult for us to make the sacrifice of ourselves that is involved in loving. Loving always asks at least this sacrifice, the orientation of my thoughts and desires toward others, and the abandonment of my own self and self-interest. Needless to say, such

*I feel the capacity to*
*CARE*
*is the thing which gives life*
*its deepest significance.*

*Pablo Casals*

abandonment always involves a high cost
to self.

But if a life of love is difficult, it is not a
bleak or unrewarding life. In fact, it is the
only truly human and happy life, for it is filled
with concerns that are as deep as life, as wide
as the whole world, and as far-reaching as
eternity. It is only when we have consented
to love, and have agreed to forget ourselves,
that we can find our fulfillment. It will come
unperceived and mysterious like the grace of
God. However, we will recognize it and it will
be recognized in us. We will have made the
Copernican revolution that relocates the
focus of our minds and hearts on the good
and fulfillment of others; and although this
conversion has sought nothing for itself, it
has received everything. The lovable person
is, in the last analysis, the one who has made
the consent and commitment to love.

So often we demand that others love us
without being willing to make the sacrifice
and abandonment of self that is necessary to
become lovable. However, if we have mas-
tered the delicate and profound paradox that
love involves, and have been willing to
dedicate ourselves without reservation or
demand for return to the needs and fulfill-

ment of others, we will certainly be loved and fulfilled within ourselves.

But how can we love if we have never been loved? Between black and white there is always an area of gray. All of us have some capacity to love, some ability to move the focus of our minds out from ourselves to the needs, happiness, and fulfillment of others. To the extent that we do this, to the extent that we actualize this potential that is latent within us, we will be loved. Even if at the beginning we can love only a little, we shall be loved a little; and the love that we receive will empower us to grow more and more out of ourselves in the directions that love leads. This, then, is the challenge that lies before each of us: we must utilize whatever capacity we have for love, be it small or great. To the extent that we are willing to make the effort and dedication that is involved, we will be nourished and strengthened by the love that we shall receive in return; but we must remember that in making this self-donation, the focus of our minds must always be away from self and this precludes thinking of or asking for a return. When we ask that question: "What have you done for me?" we have ceased to love.

# Christ and Love

Jesus our Lord left no doubt about the
credential of the Christian. He said, "I give
you a new commandment: love one another.
As I have loved you, so you also should love
one another. This is how all will know that
you are my disciples, if you have love for one
another" (John 13:34–35). Saint John
reminds us in his First Epistle that it is impossible to love God whom we do not see
and not love those around us whom we
do see.

All of these things we have read, and
perhaps we pay them more lip service than
life service. We know that Christ takes as
done to himself what we do to others. He
accepts as given to himself our concern and
kindness for others. In the daily battle,
however, when our own needs are so throbbing and painful, we forget this.

The only attitude worthy of the Christian
is that of Christ, who thought of others
always, who gave himself until he had not
another drop of blood to give. In his own
words, "No one has greater love than this, to
lay down one's life for his friends." This is,
of course, what love asks of us, that we lay

down our lives for others. Only when we
have consented to do this will we find
ourselves, our own happiness and fulfillment,
and only then will we be true Christians. If
we fail to do this, perhaps there will be some
justification in the questions that the agnostic
philosopher Nietzsche once asked: "If Christians wish us to believe in their Redeemer,
why don't they look a little more redeemed?"
It was this same Nietzsche who coined the
phrase, so sadly common in our own days:
"God is dead."

# Love of Christ
# in the Love of Christians

In the 1920s, the philosopher of American
communism was a Jew named Mike Gold.
After communism fell into general disrepute
in this country, Mike Gold became a man of
oblivion. In this oblivion he wrote a book,
*Jews without Money.* In describing his childhood in New York City, he tells of his
mother's instructions never to wander beyond four certain streets. She could not tell
him that it was a Jewish ghetto. She could not
tell him that he had the wrong kind of blood
in his veins. Children do not understand

God does not create
in order to
**acquire**
something
but in order to
**give**
something…

only to share himself.

prejudice. Prejudice is a poison that must gradually seep into a person's bloodstream.

In his narration, Mike Gold tells of the day that curiosity lured him beyond the four streets, outside of his ghetto, and of how he was accosted by a group of older boys who asked him a puzzling question: "Hey, kid, are you a *kike*?" "I don't know." He had never heard the word before. The older boys came back with a paraphrase of their question: "Are you a Christ-killer?" Again, the small boy responded, "I don't know." He had never heard that word either. So the older boys asked him where he lived, and trained like most small boys to recite their address in the case of being lost, Mike Gold told them where he lived. "So you are a kike; you are a Christ-killer. Well, you're in Christian territory and we are Christians. We're going to teach you to stay where you belong!" And so they beat the little boy, bloodied his face, tore his clothes, and sent him home to the jeering litany: "We are Christians and you killed Christ! Stay where you belong! We are Christians and you killed Christ . . ."

When he arrived home, Mike Gold was asked by his frightened mother: "What

happened to you, Mike?" He could answer
only: "I don't know." "Who did this to you,
Mike?" Again he answered: "I don't know."
And so the mother washed the blood from
the face of her little boy and put him into
fresh clothes and then she took him into her
lap as she sat in a rocker, and tried to soothe
him. Mike Gold recalled so much later in life
that he raised his small battered lips to the ear
of his mother and asked: "Mama, who is
Christ?"

Mike Gold died in 1967. His last meals
were taken at a Catholic Charity house in New
York City, run by Dorothy Day. She once
said of him: "Mike Gold eats every day at the
table of Christ, but he will probably never
accept him because of the day he first heard
his name." And so he died.

For better or for worse, Christ has taken
us as his living symbols in this world. The
world that is asking whether God is dead or
not, the world that is asking who Christ is can
find its answers only in the Christian. For
better or for worse, we are Christ to the
world.

Almost any other apologetic for the Christian faith can be memorized, rehearsed, and

delivered without effect except the apologetic of love. Love, which of its essence seeks only the good of others and is willing to pay the high price of self-forgetfulness, is a product that is hard to imitate or counterfeit.

To love, one must have enormous motivation. In a grasping world, in a world that is gouging and clawing for earthly riches, Christians by their love must stand forth as a breathtaking exception. True Christians must seek only the good, the fulfillment, and the destiny of their fellow human beings. Love will always be their most eloquent argument and effective means. It is difficult. And yet the Lord Jesus of the Gospels stands with us, and it becomes our Christian imperative: "This is how all will know that you are my disciples, if you have love for one another."

# Epilogue

The poet Archibald MacLeish has said that we are affected more by symbols than by ideas. The symbol of loneliness, he says, is two lights above the sea; the symbol of grief is a solitary figure standing in a doorway. The symbol of Christ in this world is the Christian. Over the altars of our churches there hangs a large crucifix. Under the crucifix there is the unwritten caption: "No one has greater love than this . . . love one another as I have loved you." It is a constant reminder of our vocation as witnesses to Christ.

There is a story told about the evangelist Saint John, the one who wrote "God is love.

. . . If anyone says, 'I love God,' but hates his
brother, he is a liar; for whoever does not
love a brother whom he has seen cannot love
God whom he has not seen" (1 John 5:16,
20). It is of this John that the story is told
that in the evening of his long life, he would
sit for hours with his younger disciples
gathered at his feet. One day, as it is related
in this well-established tradition, one of his
disciples complained: "John, you always talk
about love, about God's love for us and about
our love for one another. Why don't you tell
us about something else besides love?" The
evangelist, who once as a youth had laid his
head over the heart of God made man, is said
to have replied: "Because there is nothing else,
just love . . . love . . . love."

It is a long and hard road. It is an altar of
sacrifice. It asks an enormous price in
self-forgetfulness. It must seek nothing for
itself. Love is the only way to our human
destiny and to the feet of God, who is Love.